ŠEVČÍK

OPUS 2 PART 6

SCHOOL OF BOWING
TECHNIQUE

SCHULE DER
BOGENTECHNIK

ÉCOLE DU MÉCANISME
DE L'ARCHET

FOR

CELLO

ARR. FEUILLARD

BOSWORTH

№ 38.

Arpeggien auf vier Saiten.	Arpèges sur quatres cordes.	Arpeggios on four strings.
Beispiel mit 726 Varianten.	Exemple avec 726 variantes.	Example with 726 Variations.
	Arpézie na čtyřech strunách.	Арпеджіи на Четырехъ струнахъ.
	Příklad s 726 proměnami.	Примѣръ съ 726 варіантами.

Edited and translated by H. Brett. Edited by L. R. Feuillard and A. E. Bosworth.

| Varianten des vorhergehenden Bei- | Variantes sur l'exemple précédent. | Variations on the foregoing example. |
| spieles. | *Proměny předchoziho příkladu.* | Варіанты предыдущаго примѣра. |

Mit ganzem Bogen.
Tout l'archet.
Whole bow-length.
Celým smyčcet.
Цѣлымъ смычкомъ.

Mit halbem Bogen.
Moitié de l'archet.
Half bow-length.
Polovici smyčce.
Половиною смычка.

Mit der Mitte des Bogens.
Du milieu de l'archet.
Bow-middle.
Středem smyčce.
Серединою смычка.

Staccato.

4

Legato.

(Métr: ♩= 80, ♪= 96)

Veränderungen in Achteln. | Variantes en croches. | Variations in quavers (eighth-notes).
Proměny v osminách. | Изменения восьмыми.

Mit einem Drittel des Bogens. (Métr: ♩=104)
Avec un tiers de l'archet.
One third of bow-length.

Třetinou smyčce.
Одною третью смычка.

Legato. (Métr: ♩=80, ♪=96, ♬=112)

B. & C⁰ 6429

) Alle mit M bezeichneten Strichübungen in der Mitte, an der Spitze und am Frosch üben. | *) On travaillera les coups d'archet marqués de M* du milieu, de la pointe et du talon. | *) Practice the bowings marked M* at the middle, tip, and frog.
| *) Všecka značkou M* označená cvičení smyková cvič středem, u hrotu a u žabky. | *) Упражнения, обозначенныя M*, играть серединою, концомъ и у колодочки.

B. & Cº 6129

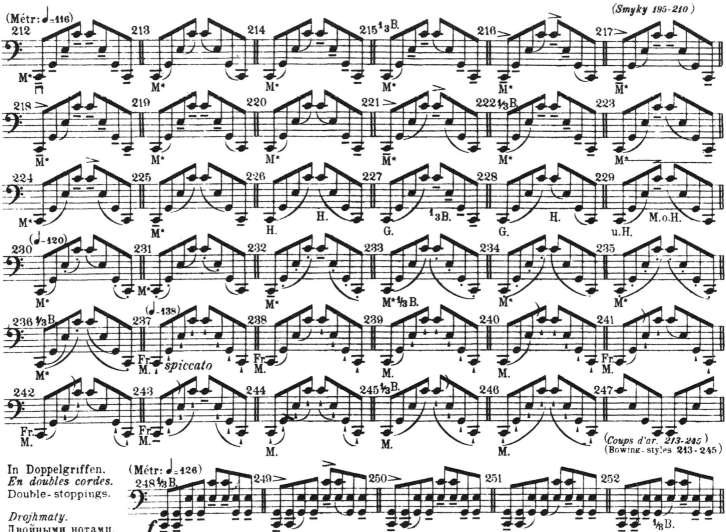

(Strichart 195-210)
(Coups d'ar. 195-210)
(Bowing-styles 195 to 210)

(Smyky 195-210)

(Coups d'ar. 213-245)
(Bowing-styles 213-245)

In Doppelgriffen.
En doubles cordes.
Double-stoppings.

Drojhmaty.
Двойными нотами.

(Strichart 249-256)
(Coups d'ar. 249-256)
(Bowing-styles 249 to 256)

(Smyky 249-256)

Veränderungen in Triolen. | Variantes en triolets. | Variations in Triplets.
Proměny triolové. | Измѣненія тріолями.

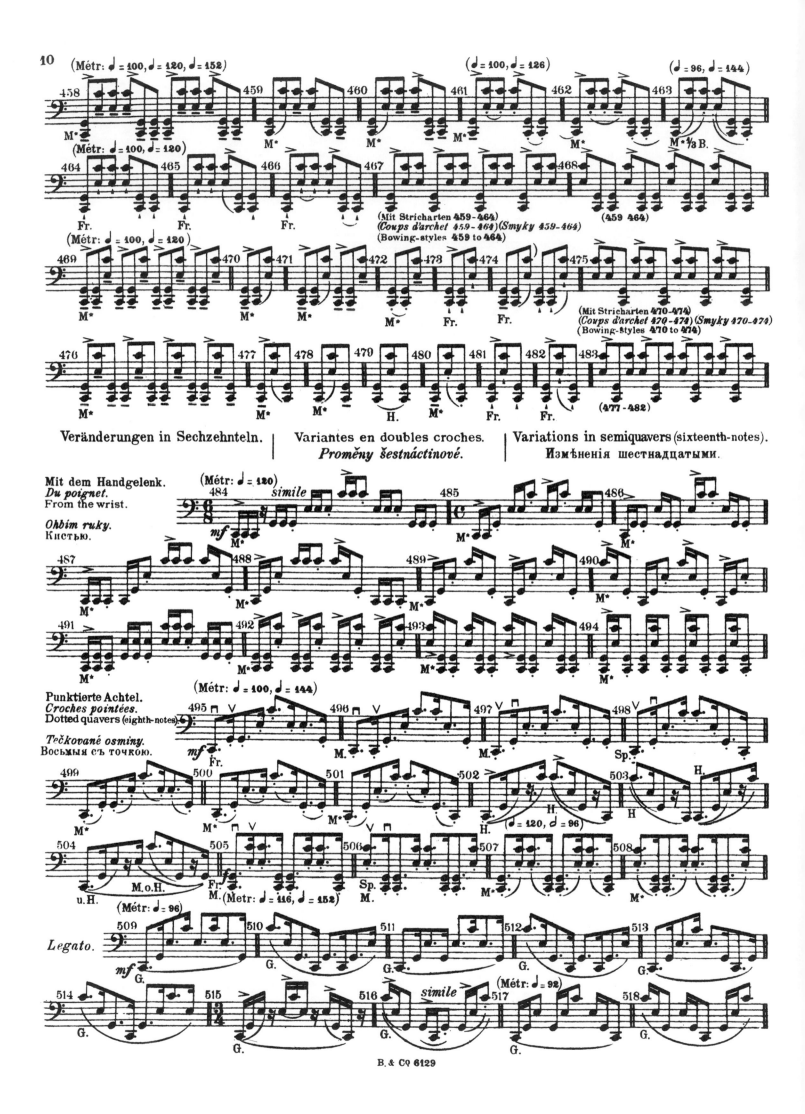

Veränderungen in Sechzehnteln. | Variantes en doubles croches. | Variations in semiquavers (sixteenth-notes).
Proměny šestnáctinové. | Изменения шестнадцатыми.

14

B. & Cº 6129

Akkorde auf 4 Saiten.
Accords sur 4 cordes.
Chords on 4 strings.

Akkordy na 4 strunách.
Аккорды на 4 струнахъ.

The Works of
OTAKAR ŠEVČÍK

VIOLIN

LITTLE SEVCIK, Elementary Tutor
SEVCIK SCALES & ARPEGGIOS
HOW TO PRACTISE SEVCIK'S MASTERWORKS
INTRODUCTION TO SEVCIK VIOLIN STUDIES
from Op. 1 (by K. W. Rokos)

For More Advanced Pupils

OP. 1. SCHOOL OF VIOLIN TECHNIQUE.
Part 1. Exercises in the 1st Position.
Part 2. Exercises in the 2nd-7th Positions.
Part 3. Exercises in Change of Position.
Part 4. Exercises in Double-Stopping, Triple-Stopping, Quadruple-Stopping (3 & 4-part chords). Pizzicato, Flageolet Tones, Harmonics.

OP. 1. Complete, bound in Cloth.

Development of the Right Hand

OP. 2. SCHOOL OF BOWING TECHNIQUE.
(4,000 Exercises in Bowing)
Parts 1-6
Exercise Themes to Op. 2.

OP. 3. 40 VARIATIONS
Piano Accompaniment (optional)

OPS. 2 & 3, Complete, bound in Cloth.

Development of the Left Hand

OP. 6. VIOLIN METHOD FOR BEGINNERS.
Parts 1-5. 1st Position.
Part 6. Studies Preparatory to the various Positions.
Part 7. 5th Position and combining the various Positions.

OP. 6. Complete, bound in Cloth.

For Slightly Advanced Pupils

OP. 7. STUDIES PREPARATORY TO THE SHAKE & DEVELOPMENT IN DOUBLE-STOPPING.
Part 1. Exercises in the 1st Position.
Part 2. Exercises in the 2nd, 3rd, 4th, 5th & 6th Positions.

OP. 8. CHANGES OF POSITION & PREPARATORY SCALE STUDIES.
In Thirds, Sixths, Octaves, & Tenths.

OP. 9. PREPARATORY STUDIES IN DOUBLE-STOPPING.
In Thirds, Sixths, Octaves & Tenths.

OPS. 7, 8 & 9. Complete, bound in Cloth.

VIOLA

Arranged by Lionel Tertis

OP. 1. SCHOOL OF TECHNIQUE.
Part 1. Exercises in the 1st Position.
Part 2. Exercises in the 2nd-7th Positions.
Part 3/4. Exercises in Changes of Position & in Double, Triple & Quadruple Stopping, etc.

OP. 2. SCHOOL OF BOWING TECHNIQUE.
Parts 1, 2 & 3.

OP. 3. FORTY VARIATIONS (arr. Margaret Major)
Piano Accompaniment (optional)

OP. 8. CHANGES OF POSITION & PREPARATORY SCALE STUDIES.

OP. 9. PREPARATORY STUDIES IN DOUBLE-STOPPING (arr. Alan Arnold)

CELLO

OP. 1. THUMB PLACING EXERCISES.
Part 1. 1st Position (arr. W. Schultz)

OP. 2. SCHOOL OF BOWING TECHNIQUE
(4,000 Exercises arr. Feuillard)
Parts 1-6.

OP. 3. 40 VARIATIONS (arr. Feuillard)
Piano Accompaniment (optional)

OP. 8. CHANGES OF POSITION & PREPARATORY SCALE STUDIES.
In Thirds, Sixths, Octaves & Tenths (arr. H. Boyd)